A New Dawn

The Power of Change

31 Topical Devotions for Daily Inspiration

Dawn S. Christopher

A New Dawn

Copyright © 2019 by Dawn S. Christopher

Cover design by EDZ Art.

Self - Published with Live on Purpose, LLC.

Manufactured in United States of America.

This book is dedicated to all of the wonderful women everywhere I've had the privilege of serving through prayer, mentorship, counseling and encouraging. You are greatly appreciated. You have inspired and ignited a flame within me that's only the beginning. My heart is burning with a desire to do more. Just know this one is for you!

A New Dawn

Table of Contents

Devotions

A New Dawn

Foreword

When I first heard Rev. Dawn S. Christopher speak, it was the occasion of a Women's Day service in a small Baptist church in Wilmington, DE more than 27 years ago. It was a warm day. I was hot and tired and could only think of the million other things I had to do when church was out. Don't judge. I'm sure you all have had days like that; when you were sitting in church, hoping God was not noticing that your attention span was far less than what it should have been, and that your every thought was neither on Him nor the scripture that had been read and punctuated with a loud "Amen". Yet, when Rev. Dawn stood up to speak, she was focused, captivating, and right on point. Her message touched the oldest to the youngest in the room.

As I read her recent offering "A New Dawn", I was catapulted back to that hot Women's Day service in the 90's. In "A New Dawn", she is once again focused in her presentation, captivating in her delivery, and she has something for every reader at every stage of her chronological life. From Dolls, Divas and Dears to the proverbial Millennials, Gen Xers and Baby Boomers; there is a devotion (many of them) here that will speak to every situation we run into in our lives. My personal favorites are "Anxiety" and "Disappointment" and "Doubt" and "Deliverance" and "Favor" and "Pressure" and "Restoration" and "Steadfast" and "Trust" and "Vision" and... oh well, I have to admit, I love them all. Read on and see if you agree that this is truly one to keep by the bedside for morning and evening meditation. Congratulations, Rev. Dawn, you've, yet again, managed to extend my really short attention span.

With much Delta love,

Karen H. Bostick

President, Wilmington (DE) Alumnae Chapter

Delta Sigma Theta Sorority, Incorporated

Preface

I wrote this devotional because God told me to. This book has been in the making for quite some time. It has been 10 years to be exact. I know it should not have taken so long, but it took a lot to bring it to fruition. Through the inspiration of the Holy Spirit, I had a desire to minister to women in a special way.

I have been the Chaplain for the Wilmington (DE) Alumnae Chapter of Delta Sigma Theta Sorority, Incorporated, for about 12 years. As a result, I realized the needs of women were great and I needed to do something. What started on a monthly basis grew into a desire to plant seeds in the lives of all women.

Through this simple devotional, I want to encourage, strengthen, renew and revive the faith of all my sisters everywhere. For those that don't know God, I want to introduce him to you and present the precious gift of salvation. For those that know him, I want you to go deeper and reach higher in your relationship.

I pray this devotional is a blessing. As you read it, I believe real life will flow through these pages and you will be able to apply the words of this book to everyday situations. There's nothing deep about it.

Simply pray and read. The Holy Spirit will speak. By faith, you will take a journey that will change your life. You will never be the same. I guarantee, at some point, you will not want to be. Peace.

The Devotional Format

Before we begin, let me share with you how to best use this devotional. For 31 days, I will inspire, encourage, and help deepen your relationship with God.

The blueprint of this book is designed to do just that. Each topic will be introduced with a definition, followed by an anecdote about our subject. Then you will be taken to the **Power of Change**.

At this point, personal reflection takes place with questions and/or statements for you to meditate upon. Afterwards, we will explore the word of God and you will see **"Let There Be Light"** at which time there will be examples for you to examine to help in your understanding.

Finally, to seal what you've received, you will see, "Let's Pray". If you are ready, Let's Begin!

Acknowledgements

Before I thank anyone, I must thank God. Thank you Lord. You have revealed something on the inside that must be shared with others. For that, I give You praise.

To my husband, Calvin, your unconditional love means more than you know. I am also aware of your undercover promotion of this ministry. You may never say it, but it's out there. To my son, Julian, thank you for loving me. I treasure our relationship. Thanks for allowing me to be your second mom. To my beautiful daughters and legacies, Tiffany and Ashley, thanks for trusting me with your heart and for those times you unknowingly ministered to me. I am proud to be your mother and "Soror". To my mother, "Sweetie", my biggest cheerleader, your faithful support and encouragement has been everything to me.

To my special sister friends, Karen, Redds, and Tonie, you've loved and prayed me through some difficult times. To Sophie, who never leaves my side, words cannot express how much you mean to me. To Elizabeth, thanks for taking the time a few years ago to review this work over and over again. It's finally here. To Regina thanks for making sure my references were documented correctly. To Max, the last prayer you prayed was the push I needed. And to Maurice Gray thanks for working with me. You're an author in your own right. I appreciate you.

Finally, to my Byrd's AME Church Family, you make me feel like I'm the best pastor in the world. To First Alliance Church and Pastor Erick Adams, thank you for making your sanctuary available for me to record my audio book. We could feel the presence of the Holy Spirit while recording! To Danielle Washington, thank you for offering your instrumental music to play behind my audio book. To Kadesha Carroll, thanks for reminding me to live on purpose. I absolutely love working with you. Last, but not least, to the wonderful ladies of the Wilmington (DE) Alumnae Chapter of Delta Sigma Theta, Sorority, Incorporated. Thanks for your love and encouragement. I am truly grateful. This is because of you. Thanks so much.

ANXIETY

Anxiety – distress or uneasiness of mind caused by fear of danger or misfortune.

Goodbye to those feelings of uneasiness that usually happen when I am fearful about something. I AM overcoming those feelings by discovering the source of the uneasiness.

The Power of Change

Are you worried about something?

_____

Is there a lack of self-confidence?

_____

Is it something you can control?

_____

Do you doubt God's ability to deliver?

_____

Are these feelings warranted?

_____

If not, what can you do differently?

_____

ANXIETY

Do not fret or have any anxiety about anything, but in every circumstance and in everything, by prayer and petition (definite requests), with thanksgiving, continue to make your wants known to God.

Philippians 4:6 (AMP)

Let There Be Light

As you read the above scripture, you may feel not having anxiety is easier said than done. Some of us operate under such high levels of stress that anxiety is all we know. The ability to function without it is difficult, as habits are not easily broken. Living without anxiety is a learned behavior. It means choosing peace and purposely deciding not to worry.

One of the main components of anxiety is fear. Fear operates on the premise of the unknown. It is a strategy of the enemy used against the people of God. When fear is in operation, it is fortified by ignorance and maintained by reinforced negatives. Through conversations, mental images, and preconceived notions, many Christians believe the worst of their circumstances. This subtle tactic causes many to make decisions based on what they think. Conclusions are drawn relative to perceptions and possibilities as opposed to reality. Unfortunately, perception of fear is bigger than the ability to overcome it.

Another component of anxiety is doubt. Doubt preys on individuals with uncertainty. They worry about pressing issues, constantly kept in a state of uneasiness. This is not the will of God. Fear and doubt contribute to anxiety in a major way. Both are designed to sabotage one's personal tranquility.

As previously mentioned, living without anxiety is a learned behavior. Daily, you must confront lurking demons that desire to tempt you into stress. Ask the following questions. What is causing anxiety? Is it a job? Are there unresolved past issues? Are you frustrated? How do you start and end the day? What are your priorities? Do you stick to them? These are just some things to consider. Once you have answered these questions, start working to resolve anxieties. Maybe your list of questions is entirely different. It doesn't matter. The important thing is to find out what's going on.

Anxiety may be caused by a number of things. We are subject to all types of pressure. However, it is our responsibility to take care of the life God has given. It's never too late to make changes. As you grow in God's grace and obey His will, change is eminent. From there, you have nothing to lose and everything to gain. You are purposed to live life free of anxiety. It is the will of God. He loves you that much!

Let's Pray!

Heavenly Father, I bow before your presence. You have been so good to me. Help me to trust you. Let your peace rest upon me. Show me how to live a stress-free life, casting my cares upon you.

In Jesus' name,
Amen

AUTHORITY

Authority – The right to control, command, or determine.

The existence of authority is the creation of an almighty God. He is the ultimate authority and the source of it all. Because He is the source of it all, as His children, we have access to it. But having access means nothing, if you don't take advantage of it. If you're going to have a precise understanding of authority, you must be certain it goes way beyond the scope of telling someone what to do.

The Power of Change

Do you have a clear understanding of authority?

_____

_____

_____

_____

Is it simply the ability to be in control, or is there more?

_____

_____

_____

_____

AUTHORITY

Listen carefully: I have given you authority [that you now possess] to tread on serpents and scorpions, and [the ability to exercise authority] over all the power of the enemy (Satan); and nothing will [in any way] harm you.

Luke 10:19 (AMP)

Let There Be Light

First and foremost, God is the source of **all** authority. It rests, rules, and abides with Him. That means heavenly and earthly authority. The scripture reference serves as a good reminder. As a result, God has the power to determine when, and how, authority operates; and also with whom.

Secondly, many Christians unknowingly suffer because they have missed the fact that authority begins and ends with God. Consequently, they're at a loss in many situations, and fail to realize there's also power to go along with the authority. Yes, power and authority are co-laborers together. The two go hand in hand. It's one thing to have authority (influence). It's another to have the power (potential) to exert it. Operating in authority with no power is like commanding "Alexa" without a power source. You'll give the order, but she won't respond. There must be a power source. For you, that power comes from God. He has given it to you!

Thirdly, now that you know power and authority are yours, what are you going to do with them? It's time to make a decision. The next move is yours. Make sure, like "Alexa", you're plugged into your power source. That way, you will no longer be subject to the wiles of the enemy without recourse. Put a stop to the battering ram of satanic badgering and send out a cease and desist order against all attacks.

Finally, want real change? Then **you** make the difference in your **own** life. Stop settling for any, and every, hand dealt your way. Speak the Word! Stand in your God-given authority, and don't flinch. Now, read the above scripture again. What does it say? Do you believe it? If you do, walk in it! You're one step of faith away from dismantling the weaponry of the enemy; uprooting the spirit of sabotage; and tearing down strongholds. Remember, you're in charge, not Satan. Got authority?

Let's Pray!

Heavenly Father, You are sovereign. You have given us all power and authority over the works of the enemy. Today, I walk in that power and authority. Today, I serve an eviction notice to the enemy. Today, I speak Your Word with expectation. Today, I prevail, and declare my enemies are scattered.

In Jesus' name,
Amen

A New Dawn

CHANGE

Change – to put or take in place of something else; substitute; replace with; transfer to another of similar kind; switch; alter; pass from one place to another.

Change is a natural part of life. It happens every day. In order to grow, we must be ready to change. Don't be afraid to try something new or different. If it doesn't work, try something else. You have nothing to lose.

The Power of Change

Do you tend to resist change?

_____

_____

When is the last time that you tried something new?

_____

_____

Why are you so afraid of the unknown?

_____

_____

CHANGE

Therefore, if any man be in Christ, he is a new creature: old things are passed away; behold all things become new.

2 Corinthians 5:17 (KJV)

Let There Be Light

The subject of change is very interesting. To some, it's exciting; something to look forward to. To others, it's not. Fear and dread come upon them. Most people don't like change because change means doing something different; something you may not want to do. "Why can't things stay the same?" you ask. A songwriter once said, "**Everything must change. Nothing stays the same.**" The fact is, change is imminent and can be good. If it takes you out of complacency, and thrusts you into a new situation, which helps you learn more about yourself; it's beneficial. That's what's so awesome about being in Christ.

From a spiritual perspective, to be in Christ is a position. Webster's Dictionary says position is placement, an arrangement, attitude, posture, and a disposition. God has a position for you. It was arranged before the foundations of the world. How do you get into this position? You must be totally sold out to God. He wants a yielded vessel that understands, *"For In Him we live and move and have our being."* (Acts 17:28, NIV) One that does *"Trust in the Lord with all thine heart and lean not unto thine own understanding. In all thy ways acknowledge Him and He will direct thy paths."*

(Proverbs 3:5-6, KJV) From this, we learn that Christ will direct us. Through Christ's direction, an inner leading follows. God makes all things new. These new things are opportunities to bring dreams, visions, and desires, locked up in imagination, into reality.

It's time to get ready. It's time to bring forth the new creature in Christ. It's time for your purpose to come to pass. Everything you're destined to be now comes to life. Everything! As the saying goes, *"Nothing missing, nothing broken."*

Know this. At some point in life, you *will* face change. Your response to it, greatly determines the outcome you receive. Your acceptance of it, determines the legacy you leave behind. Get ready. Let God have His way. Change is coming!

Let's Pray!

Lord God. You are the creator of all things, the giver of every good and perfect gift. My change is in Your hands. Help me to accept it. Help me to leave the past behind. Teach me the new way to live.

In Jesus' name,
Amen

A New Dawn

<u>COURAGE</u>

Courage – the quality of mind or spirit that enables a person to face difficulty, danger, pain, etc., without fear; bravery.

Stepping into the unknown can be overwhelming. It takes a lot to speak up, face conflict, and take a stand. There's always hesitancy if you've never done it before. Ask God to help you. You can do it. You're much stronger than you think!

The Power of Change

Is there something in your life that you have been avoiding?

_____

_____

If you answered yes, why have you avoided it for so long?

_____

_____

If you do not complete this task, will you be satisfied with your life?

_____

_____

COURAGE

This is my command – be strong and courageous! Do not be afraid or discouraged. For the Lord your God is with you wherever you go.

Joshua 1:9 (NLT)

Let There Be Light

Moses died. Joshua was the new leader of the children of Israel. As successor, it was time for him to take up the mantle, and lead Israel to the Promised Land. God told Joshua to be strong and courageous. His faith and obedience would see him through.

Like Joshua, we too are called to be strong and courageous. Many obstacles will challenge our ability to be strong, as we face difficult situations. Knowing God is present helps us to persevere as we progress toward His promises.

God makes promises only He can keep. Some of these promises seem utterly impossible. Life's journey brings many twists and turns, and we cannot imagine how these promises will come to pass. However, know this; although there is adversity, we must believe and be courageous, to receive the promises of God.

God's instruction to Joshua to be strong and courageous was not a request. It was a command. He could not allow him to operate in fear. Fear would impede the plan of God for Joshua's life.

As God was with Joshua, so is He with you. He hasn't changed. ***God is the same yesterday, today, and forever.*** At times, it may be difficult. Remember God's words to Joshua. Recall them as often as necessary. Be strong and do not be afraid.

Let's Pray!

Praises to You, Almighty God! You are holy, righteous and all powerful. I come to You for strength and courage. Help me to stand in the midst of opposition. Bless me to fear nothing, and no one, but You. Help me to trust Your promises. Thank you for never leaving me. I am grateful for Your faithfulness.

In Jesus' name,
Amen

A New Dawn

DELIVERANCE

Deliverance – setting free; rescue; release.

Feeling stuck in the same old thing can be discouraging. If you're not careful, you'll think you can't do anything else. Don't get tricked. Many have felt this way, but made a decision not to stay there. Choose to get out. God specializes in stuck. He always provides a way of escape.

The Power of Change

Think honestly. What is one thing that you would like to be delivered (set free) from?

_____

_____

_____

_____

Who or what has you going around in the same circle?

_____

_____

_____

_____

DELIVERANCE

The angel of the Lord encampeth round about them that fear him, and delivereth them. Many are the afflictions of the righteous; but the Lord delivereth him out of them all.

Psalm 34:7, 19 (KJV)

Let There Be Light

When thinking of deliverance, the image of a caged bird comes to mind. Birds are beautiful creatures formed by the hand of God. By nature, most of them are designed to fly. Their wings are instruments constructed for aviation. Through them, birds handle wind velocity, and reach high altitudes. At times, they can fly at certain levels for periods of time, until landing is possible. Flying is freedom. But, for a caged bird, it is impossible. They are restricted. The cage and bird are not designed to operate together. They are complete opposites.

We are God's most prized creation; shaped in His image and likeness, fashioned for greatness. Yet, many don't have a clue to what God has given us the ability to do. We are affected by family history, orientation, culture, background, tradition, experiences, and exposure. These things can be like the cage, restricting our progress. As a result, we are like the caged bird.

Like the caged bird, we've been created by God to fly; but because of restrictions, movement has been limited. These limitations may be walls of opposition, or our own fears, worries, and doubts from being caged so long. What must we do? We must make a decision to move forward. With gifts, skills, talents, and abilities, the only way to release them is through an open cage; a cage we must open.

For the bird, freedom is gained through an unlocked cage. For you, it's a matter of being tired of being caged. You must tire of being agitated, frustrated, wishing, hoping, and desiring to be set free. The scripture reference says God provides for your deliverance. In the most unusual circumstances, He can, and will, make a way. God hears the cries of His people. Through patience, faith, prayer, and the Word, He will remove all obstacles out of the way.

Your opportunity to be set free has come. Herein lies your chance to fly. Step out so you can come out. Come out of fear! Come out of worry! Come out of doubt! This is a mandate, not a request. Come out! Christ has set you free!

Let's Pray!

Great God. Today, I pray for deliverance. Help me to fly like a bird. Help me to soar to the highest heights and navigate the deepest depths. Lead me down freedom's path and let Your glory shine upon me.

In Jesus' name,
Amen

A New Dawn

DESTINY

Destiny – the seemingly inevitable or necessary succession of events; fate; supernatural agency.

Feeling restless? The discomfort you feel is the Holy Spirit tugging at you. It's His way of trying to redirect your steps. He's trying to get your attention. He's trying to tell you something. God has a plan for you. He wants you to discover it.

The Power of Change

Are you excited about your future?

_____

_____

_____

Do you feel a tug for something bigger on the horizon?

_____

_____

_____

Do you believe God has great plans for you? If no, why not?

_____

_____

_____

DESTINY

For I know the plans I have for you, says the Lord. They are plans for good and not for evil, to give you a future and a hope.

Jeremiah 29:11 (LB)

Let There Be Light

As I prepared to write, I thought about a conversation I had a few years ago with my daughter. At the time, she had only been working on her job three months and had three promotions. This job was unexpected. She was not interested in looking for a new job, but a series of events led to looking for employment elsewhere.

Before my daughter's employment, we prayed for guidance. Making phone calls, searching the Internet, and checking classified ads became her routine. However, a conversation with an old friend provided a lead.

It's interesting to see the hand of God at work in our lives. The Bible says, *"The steps of a good man are ordered by the Lord and He delighteth in his way."* (Psalm 37:23, KJV) Subsequently, my daughter received a blessing.

This is how God works in our lives. The way He has planned will consist of many experiences. The Bible says, *"And we know that all things work together for good to them that love God, to them who are the called according to His purpose."* (Romans 8:28, KJV) God has a plan. The outcome is good, not evil. There is a process, with much to learn along the way; but through this, you will mature in the faith, and bring glory and honor to God.

The way may be difficult. At times, it will seem like you're falling. You won't. **With God you will land on your feet. Great potential calls for a great process.** There's no easy way, and no coincidences. Like the Apostle Paul, learn not to kick against the pricks. Stop fighting and go with the flow. God will grant the grace to reach the place called destiny.

Destiny is where your mark is made in this world. It is the place where purpose is found. It gives meaning to your very existence. Your assignment is found in your destiny; as well as in whom, and what, you're assigned to. Once reached, it will no longer be known as just the place of destiny. It will be identified as the place of ongoing accomplishment, where *"...He which hath begun a good work in you will perform it until the day of Jesus Christ."* (Philippians 1:6, KJV)

DESTINY. DESTINY PURSUED. DESTINY ACCOMPLISHED. DESTINY FULFILLED!!!

Let's Pray!

Lord I worship You. You are God of Your Word. I'm Yours Lord; help me to walk in Your perfect will. Show me Your plan for my life. Help me cooperate with Your Spirit. Let Your purpose be fulfilled in me. Thank you Lord.

In Jesus' name,
Amen

<u>DISAPPOINTMENT</u>

Disappoint - to fail to fulfill expectations or wishes of; thwart; frustrate.

So things didn't work out the way you desired. Please don't give up. It's not over yet. Perhaps it wasn't the right time. Trust God. Your timing is in His hands.

The Power of Change

When was the last time you were disappointed?

_____

_____

How did it make you feel?

_____

_____

What did you do with those feelings? How did you overcome?

_____

_____

> ## DISAPPOINTMENT
>
> And we know that all things work together for good to them that love God, to them who are the called according to His purpose.
>
> ### Romans 8:28 (KJV)

Let There Be Light

Can you imagine never being disappointed? Can you imagine never being frustrated or hurt? Sounds wonderful, but that's not real life. Real life is full of disappointment, frustration, and hurt. It's how you respond that makes the difference.

Some people believe disappointment equates to failure. They feel they've done something wrong. But, doing something wrong may not be the case. While some disappointments are due to a lack of patience, or premature decisions, that's not true in all situations. Sometimes disappointments come from being too dependent on someone, or something, for your own personal success.

Disappointment does not always have to be something negative. Sometimes it serves to steer us in the right direction. In other words, some ideas sound wonderful, and some things look good; but thorough examination and a closer look, often reveal something altogether different.

Here's the lesson: *Nothing is as it seems.* Emotions can magnify hurt to alarming proportions. But know your hurt is bigger to you, than everyone else. Truth is, everybody is not concerned about you. I know it seems harsh, but don't allow the enemy to convince you to think your problems are the topic of everyone else's conversation. Don't allow the few people familiar with your situation to multiply in your mind to everyone. It just *ain't* so!

Don't get me wrong. You will be disappointed. Some people will know about it. However, it's not the end of the world. Learn to deal with it in a healthy manner. Don't live in the "*what ifs*". It is what it is. Just make a point to move forward. As you do, stay encouraged, and don't rely on others for your happiness or success. **You** make that happen. Disappointments may come, and disappointments may go; but they should not define you. At times, they can be helpful; and sometimes they are the true litmus test for determining your victory.

Let's Pray!

Dear God. Here I am. There's none like You in all the earth. I need Your Spirit. Help me through this disappointment. Enable me to see the truth of the matter. Reveal the lesson to be learned. Let victory be the result, despite how I feel. Help me to trust You in all things.

In Jesus' name,
Amen

DOUBT

Doubt – uncertain in opinion or belief; undecided; inclined to disbelief; question; hesitate.

Getting things done in a timely manner can be frustrating. Wondering how it's going to happen is worse. Don't worry. It will all work out, even if it's not the way you thought.

The Power of Change

Where has doubt crept in?

_____

_____

_____

_____

Is God your source? Do you believe that He will provide?

_____

_____

_____

_____

DOUBT

For he that wavereth is like a wave of the sea driven with the wind and tossed. For let not that man think he shall receive anything of the Lord. A double-minded man is unstable in all his ways.

James 1:6b – 8 (KJV)

Let There Be Light

Several years ago, my husband and I took a much-needed vacation to the Caribbean. We traveled to the island of St. Lucia. It was an all-inclusive spa facility, designed to provide personal services during the entire stay. We had everything from soup to nuts. It was truly a blessing.

Upon arrival, I felt like I was on Fantasy Island. At any moment, I expected a little man to come running out hollering, "De Plane! De Plane!" It was fabulous. Our room was right off the beach; and there were white terry cloth robes, laid out on the bed with beautiful orangey red hibiscus flowers arrayed on top. I felt like I was in Paradise.

I love the beach. It's my favorite getaway place, especially in tropical environments. The atmosphere is tranquil; and the fresh air, sun, and songs of the birds are therapeutic. I have fallen asleep on the beach many times. During those times, all was well with the world. But that didn't last forever. Sometimes tranquility can be disturbed. At any moment, it can change. And that's exactly what happened.

At that time, we weren't familiar with hurricane season. Within four days, the beautiful weather turned in another direction. Nature was preparing for a storm. Winds began to increase from a soft breeze, to a gust, causing a drop-in temperature. All sailing stopped; boats were tied down, and water activities were discontinued.

In a matter of a few days, our trip changed from Fantasy Island to Survivor. Heavy rains fell, bringing torrential downpours. Anchored boats swayed uncontrollably from side to side. The ideal vacation was no more. The order of the day became getting off the island. But flights were cancelled, and it became unsafe to leave. We had to ride out the storm at the resort.

My husband was especially worried and became very anxious. He had to get our son off to college. This was to be his freshman year. Stuck on the island, with several things on his plate, my husband doubted our son would make it to school on time. He worried. I prayed. Prompted by the Holy Spirit, I called my mother. Thank God, she took care of everything. Our son settled in school peacefully, and a few days later, we were able to go home.

So much was learned from the St. Lucia experience. Life can change in an instant. When it does, God doesn't want you to worry. He wants you to rest in Him. He's more than able to handle every problem that comes your way. Just as God carried us through the storm and worked everything out; He'll do the same for you. All He needs is a chance. Won't you trust Him?

Let's Pray!

Great Jehovah. You are the creator of all things, the giver of every good and perfect gift. Let Your Word dwell richly in me. Help me recall Your Word when the storms of life test my faith. Let Your Spirit remind me of past blessings, as I ride out the issues of life.

In Jesus' name,
Amen

FAITH

Faith – unquestioning belief that does not require proof of evidence; complete trust, confidence, or reliance.

Believe it or not, every day you live by faith. It is a gift from God. He has given you the ability to believe in something you can't see, yet trust it exists. Faith says it is so despite not being tangible.

The Power of Change

What is your faith temperature?

_____

_____

_____

_____

What do you believe God for right now?

_____

_____

_____

_____

FAITH

What is faith? It is the confident assurance that something we want is going to happen. It is the certainty that what we hope for is waiting for us, even though we cannot see it up ahead.

Hebrews 11:1 (LB)

Let There Be Light

Everyone has faith. Each day it's put to work, whether you realize it or not. It takes faith to have a bank account, drive a car, eat at restaurants, go to work, and sleep at night. These are all different examples of faith. Out of all the examples of faith, the most important, but not mentioned, is faith in God.

The above scripture says faith is confident assurance. When you are confident, you are certain what you believe is so. You are not moved by what you see, hear, or feel. You have real faith. **REAL FAITH IS NOT BASED UPON NATURAL SENSES**. Real faith means believing without seeing.

When my children were young, they played a game called Trust. The object of the game was to pair up with someone, turn with your back facing them, close your eyes, and fall backward. The person you paired up with was supposed to catch you. As you can imagine, there were many trial runs in this game.

It is the same with God. He wants our unconditional trust. There are many situations you will blindly fall into. You will have to trust God to catch you. The same fear my children had, you will have too. As with them, there will be several practice runs before you fully trust God.

God has consistently demonstrated His ability to keep us in any situation or circumstance. Yet, many still don't believe. What's the excuse? The excuse is the issue of **control. Yes, control.** Everything is fine as long as you call the shots. This should not be so. Learn to trust God and His infinite wisdom. It's liberating, and takes the limits off Him.

The moment you understand who God is, will be the moment you walk in the greatest dimension of faith imaginable. What dimension of faith is this? It is the depth, length, and width dimension of faith. It is the faith of no holds barred. It is faith where anything is possible. It is faith that *moves mountains, perseveres through adversity, slays giants, intimidates the enemy, causes the sun to stand still and turns water into wine.* It is faith that cries with a loud voice, *"Therefore I say unto you, What things soever ye desire, when ye pray, believe that ye receive them, and ye shall have them."* (Mark 11:24, KJV) By this, you know beyond a shadow of doubt, **something you want is going to happen; what you hope for is waiting for you; and what He promised, He shall perform.** This is faith. This is **real faith.**

Let's Pray!

God of Grace and Glory. You are merciful. Help me to be a living example of faith to those who don't know You. Let the light of your Spirit shine wherever I go. Let your glory speak when I'm in the presence of others. Let rivers of faith overtake them and exalt Your name.

In Jesus' name,
Amen

<u>FAVOR</u>

Favor – good will; approval; unfair partiality.

You were chosen for a reason. Stop asking why, and say why not? Your gifts, skills, and talents serve a purpose. Someone needs you. Thank God He's chosen you for such a time as this.

The Power of Change

When was the last time that you saw favor operate in your life?

_____

_____

_____

_____

Is there someone right now that you could extend favor to?

_____

_____

_____

_____

FAVOR

For thou, LORD, wilt bless the righteous; with favour wilt thou compass him as with a shield.

Psalm 5:12 (KJV)

Let There Be Light

Many believers don't understand favor. Most think favor is first in line, the best theater seats, or winning the lottery. That's not favor. Favor is much more. Favor is the hand of God upon someone's life to glorify His name. The Bible reveals a great example of favor in the story of Job. Some will disagree. But, look again at the definition of favor. It lines up with Job.

The first definition of favor is *good will.* Job experienced good will in two ways. First, the good will of God was extended towards him. God blessed Job. He had a great family, and great wealth. He was described as *"perfect and upright; one that feared God and eschewed evil."* (Job 1:1, KJV)

Second, we see the good will of Job towards others. Job shunned evil. The Bible says when his children gathered for celebrations, Job rendered special burnt offerings unto the Lord, in case they sinned. These character traits not only caught the attention of God, they appealed to Him. They became a sweet-smelling savor to His nostrils. As a result, Job won the *approval* of God; the second definition of favor.

God thought highly of Job. The Bible says, **"Now there was a day when the sons of God came to present themselves before the LORD, and Satan came also among them. And the LORD said unto Satan, whence comest thou? Then Satan answered the LORD, and said, from going to and fro in the earth, and from walking up and down in it."** (Job 1:6-7, KJV) Satan was on the prowl looking for someone to attack. God knew and told him to consider Job. **"And the LORD said unto Satan, hast thou considered my servant Job, that there is none like him in the earth, perfect and upright man, one that feareth God, and escheweth evil?"** (Job 1:8, KJV) Why would God do that? It makes no sense. However, the Bible says, **"For who hath known the mind of the Lord?" or who hath been his counsellor?"** (Romans 11:34, KJV)

There is a plan and a purpose behind every decision God makes. His motive was to promote Job and demonstrate the power of His grace. In order to do so, Job had to be tested, and God had to put His reputation on the line. This brings us to the third part of the definition of favor, **_unfair partiality_**, undeserved preference for one person or thing over another.

God demonstrated unfair partiality toward Job. His friends didn't recognize it as favor. They questioned the possibility of hidden sin in Job's life. But God knew Job's heart. He knew the outcome of the test.

God permitted Satan to destroy Job's possessions, but he was not to touch Job. **_Know this, when moments of testing_** *come, Satan must have God's permission. He is not free to move at his own discretion.* Job remained faithful. Satan was not convinced. Then God offered Job a second time; with Satan wagering skin for skin. God allowed Satan to touch Job, but not kill him. Job cried to God, but would not speak against Him. Job suffered much. Twice he was tested. Twice he persevered. He lost family, possessions, and support of friends. However, because of obedience, God blessed Job abundantly. His anointing increased through his trial; his prayers brought deliverance to his friends; and he received double for his losses.

Consequently, God was glorified, and His favor was more evident on Job's life.

Let's Pray!

All glory to the Most High God! Honor belongs to You. You have promised favor upon Your children. Let the spirit of favor shine upon my endeavors. Help me to accomplish Your will. Be magnified in the sweet victories won for the Kingdom, and let Your Name be ever praised.

In Jesus' name,
Amen

<u>FEAR</u>

Fear – something that causes feelings of dread or apprehension; something a person is afraid of; reverential awe, especially toward God.

Don't let fear of the unknown hinder you. The way to overcome it is to do the very thing that makes you afraid. Move forward with knees knocking, and heart pounding. Fear must not control you. You must control the fear.

The Power of Change

What are you afraid of?

_____

_____

_____

_____

What's causing you to delay progress?

_____

_____

_____

_____

FEAR

For I the LORD thy God will hold thy right hand, saying unto thee, fear not; I will help thee.

Isaiah 41:13 (KJV)

Let There Be Light

One of the most consistent weapons of Satan is fear. It is a spirit sent by him to steal, kill, and destroy. Fear invades the mind, creating false images. An acronym I learned for fear is **F**alse **E**vidence **A**ppearing **R**eal. Fear operates from the outside in. We are not born with it. The Apostle Paul said to Timothy, **"For God has not given us a spirit of fear; but of power, love, and a sound mind."** (2 Timothy 1:7, NKJV)

Many people are introduced to fear at an early age. It comes from horror movies, spooky stories, celebration of Halloween, adults threatening children to get good behavior, and taunts from playmates about the unknown.

I remember a game played by many children called "Bloody Mary". The idea of the game was to go into the bathroom at night and turn off the lights. The person in the bathroom was expected to stand in the mirror and shout Bloody Mary three times. Bloody Mary was supposed to appear. No one ever stayed long enough to see Bloody Mary. Each victim came running out of the bathroom because of what they thought would happen.

42

Satan wants to do the same thing to you. He wants to send you running. He wants you to find it impossible to trust God. As a result, he constantly devises plans to stop you from receiving the blessings of God.

God doesn't want you in fear. He has equipped you to effectively stand against it. You have His Word, power, authority, blood, and spirit to stand strong. These things, along with prayer, can accomplish much. The Bible says, **"The effectual and fervent prayers of a righteous man availeth much"**. (James 5:16b, KJV) God also does not want fear to rule your spirit. Do not allow yourself to engage in activities that open doors to the spirit of fear. Watch out for entertainment that employs fear; and most of all, stay away from the occult. The occult is dark and focuses on control through fear tactics. Give no place to the devil. Resist him.

As you apply wisdom in these areas, you are certain to have power over the enemy. It doesn't mean fear won't come, but you'll know how to stand. Hear the word of the LORD concerning this matter. **"Fear thou not; for I am with thee; be not dismayed for I am thy God; I will strengthen thee; yea, I will help thee; yea, I will uphold thee with the right hand of my righteousness."** (Isaiah 41:10, KJV)

Let's Pray!

Heavenly King. I bow before Your presence. Thank you for surrounding me with protection. Thank you for arms of safety. Help me not to fear. Help me to remember fear is not from You. I have no need to fear. You are ever present. All praises to You the Most High God!

In Jesus' Name,
Amen

FORGET

Forget – to lose from the mind; fail to recall; unable to remember, neglect intentionally.

Sometimes it's good to forget. You don't want to spend your time focusing on negatives. Focus on positive things. Allow these things to overshadow everything else. You must look ahead. Better days are coming.

The Power of Change

What do you need to forget? What grudge(s) are you holding onto?

_____

_____

_____

_____

Is anything holding you back from making progress?

_____

_____

_____

_____

> ### FORGET
>
> No dear brothers and sisters, I have not achieved it, but I focus on this one thing: Forgetting the past and looking to what lies ahead, I press on to reach the end of the race and receive the heavenly prize for which God, through Christ Jesus, is calling us.
>
> ### Philippians 3:13-14 (NLT)

Let There Be Light

At some time or another, you have forgotten something. It can happen at the most inopportune moment. From rushing out of the house without keys; to leaving the store and forgetting bags; it has happened to the best of us. Interestingly, forgetting can be good or bad, easy or difficult. It's good when it works in your favor. It's bad when it works against you. Then there are those times when you forget what you want to remember and remember what you want to forget.

The Bible says to forget what's behind and press towards the new. There's nothing wrong with remembering. It is a gift from God; particularly when it concerns His promises. But, God doesn't want you to stay in the same place. Constantly looking at the past can distort your focus. It can hinder God and cause you to miss great opportunities.

The Word of God says to forget the past. Yes, forget. Victories and failures of the past must be left there. They are over. If you don't leave victories behind, you'll feel there are no more to come. Failures must be forgotten because the memories of them will hinder present or future possibilities. Now is the time to press forward. Don't let anyone or anything get in the way. Seek God's help. You will make it. KEEP PRESSING.

Let's Pray!

Dear Lord, Today, I thank you for helping me to forget the past. I'm grateful it has no bearing on my future. Help me to press forward. Help me to stay focused. Use me as an example to help others. Thank you, God.

In Jesus' name,
Amen

A New Dawn

<u>FORGIVE</u>

Forgive – to give up resentment against or the desire to punish; pardon; stop being angry with; cancel or remit a debt.

We can be hurt by anyone. It's something we have no control over. However, we do have the power to forgive. Restoring others to their rightful place is biblical. Why not let God heal you both?

The Power of Change

List the names of the persons that you need to forgive.

(Feel free to use an additional sheet of paper.)

_____

_____

_____

_____

Be specific on what/ why you need to forgive.

_____

_____

_____

_____

FORGIVE

For if you forgive people their trespasses [their reckless and willful sins, leaving them, letting them go, and giving up resentment], your heavenly Father will also forgive you. But, if you do not forgive others their trespasses [their reckless and willful sins, leaving them, letting them go, and giving up resentment], neither will your Father forgive you your trespasses.

Matthew 6:14-15 (AMP)

Let There Be Light

Saying I forgive you is one of the easiest things to do. Actually, forgiving someone is another story. Practicing the art of forgiveness can be challenging. Countless times we have encountered situations that call for releasing someone from hurting us. At times, it can be so minute that we do not remember the wrong done. Or it can be so life changing only time and years will heal the wounds. Conversely, there are others who are holding us hostage, and need to practice forgiveness. More often than not, we are not even aware of what happened.

I have learned over the years that exercising forgiveness can be a blessing. It is healthy for the spirit, soul, and body. From a spiritual perspective, you are obedient to the will of God, as He requires we live peaceably with all. If you are living peaceably, the mind is not anxiety ridden, consistently worrying. If you're not worrying, you can avoid headaches, upset stomach, and other medical conditions. Now ask yourself is it worth it not to forgive?

Scripture tells us to forgive, so that we may be forgiven. God requires we forgive one another in order to live life abundantly. Abundant life is happiness, peace, and joy in the Holy Ghost.

I realize some situations are really trying. Many times, we feel justified not to forgive, based on how we've have been mistreated. However, never let anything, or anybody, have that kind of control over you. It may seem difficult at first, but through prayer, faith in God, and His Word, you can make it. Each day will be better than the day before. Believe it. Once you believe and receive it, you will be able to live it.

Let's Pray!

Dear Lord. You are wonderful. Today I give thanks for Your forgiveness. Because of Jesus, You have accepted me. Help me to forgive others and look upon them with the love and light of Your Spirit. Let forgiveness continually flow from my life that I may walk in the liberty of Christ.

In Jesus' name,
Amen

HEALING

Heal – sound, well, or healthy again; restore to health.

Sickness can occur at any given time. It doesn't notify you in advance. The good news is healing can be yours. God has given us His Word. Receive His promise of healing. His Word will make the difference.

The Power of Change

What area of your life needs healing?

_____

_____

_____

_____

Is there someone else that you can pray for healing while you wait on the manifestation of your own?

_____

_____

_____

_____

> ## HEALING
>
> Beloved, I wish above all things that thou mayest prosper and be in health even as thy soul prospereth.
>
> ### 3 John 1:2 (KJV)

Let There Be Light

Sickness is **not** the will of God. He desires wholeness in every area of your life. Sadly, most people don't know, and even more disheartening, do not believe. Why? Some find it easier to believe sickness is a regular part of life.

The above scripture speaks to the will of God. As one of His children, you are called to live by faith. Living by faith means **believing in** God and **believing** God. The two are not the same. Many believe there is a God, but don't believe what He says.

It's up to every believer to trust God for healing. Once you decide to believe, don't allow anyone or any circumstance to shake your faith. Stand firm and be matter of fact concerning your belief.

Next, be purposeful, and take necessary steps to care for your physical body. Be mindful that proper nutrition and exercise are important. Also, you must feed your spirit everything God says about healing in His Word. What does this mean? It means to read and meditate on God's word. Don't allow your mind to determine what is accepted or rejected. Seek God for revelation and understanding. He wants you well

54

informed. It's been said that *healing is the children's bread*. In other words, as a child of God you have a right to expect God to heal you.

From this point, move forward. Focus on walking by faith for your healing. Make it a point to apply it to your life. Rejoice in His will for you. It will change your life forever.

Let's Pray!

Jehovah Rapha, You are The Lord our Healer. Thank you that healing belongs to the children of God. I renounce all sickness and disease in my life. I decree and declare I am healed. It is Your will. I receive it now.

In Jesus' name,
Amen

A New Dawn

<u>INTEGRITY</u>

Integrity – adherence to moral and ethical principles; soundness of moral character; honesty.

No matter what, do the right thing. Disregard the thoughts and opinions of others who may speak otherwise. What is your heart saying? What does God require? He will never lead you wrong. Doing what's right is always best.

The Power of Change

How are you showing up at work, in your family, or at church?

Do you consider yourself as one with integrity?

_____

_____

_____

_____

When was the last time you compromised your morals? What can you do differently next time?

_____

_____

_____

_____

> ### INTEGRITY
>
> And you yourself must be an example to them by doing good works of every kind. Let everything you do reflect the integrity and seriousness of your teaching.
>
> ### Titus 2:7 (NLT)

Let There Be Light

My mother was a single parent. Growing up, we lived with my grandparents. They were good people, not perfect, but good people.

One of the things I admired most about my grandparents was how they cared for others. Helping others was constant. At anytime, you would find them feeding the hungry, clothing the naked, caring for the sick; as well as, counseling and teaching those they served. It didn't matter about color or ethnicity. To my grandparents, people were people. Everyone deserved to be respected. As a result, I learned to accept people of all cultures.

Out of all the work that my grandparents did for others, the most important thing they did was establish trust. My grandparents were very trustworthy. They didn't gossip. They cared about the people they served. They walked in integrity and it showed in all they did.

Integrity is vital to good character. It's a trait earnestly to be desired. Without it, you will not be trusted or respected. Everyone wants to be able to trust someone. Examine your life.

Make sure integrity is associated with your name. If not, now is the time to establish it. You want others to know you can be trusted.

Now, ponder the following -- are you forthright in your dealings with others? Are your motives pure and selfless? Is your word your bond? Can you be trusted to act in confidentiality? If you answered "No" to any of these questions, make the necessary changes to garner your reputation. It's not too late. By doing so, you stand the chance to leave a legacy of truth and integrity behind. This legacy will speak, and its voice will be heard for many generations to come.

Let's Pray!

Lord, You are good. You have taught me to walk uprightly and honor the words from my lips. Help me to be consistent in what I say and do. Help me to do what is right according to Your will.

In Jesus' name,
Amen

PATIENCE

Patience – the will or ability to wait or endure without complaint; steadiness endurance, or perseverance in performing a task; forbearing; tolerant; calmly tolerating; delay.

Having patience is not always easy. It's often required when you feel you don't have it to give. Many situations will come and try your patience. Ask yourself if it's worth stressing over. Patience helps you to receive the best possible outcome. But, you must wait for it.

The Power of Change

What area of your life requires the most patience right now?

_____

_____

_____

_____

How has God been patient with you?

_____

_____

_____

_____

PATIENCE

Knowing this, that the trying of your faith worketh patience. But let patience have her perfect work, that ye may be perfect and entire, wanting nothing.

James 1:3-4 (KJV)

Let There Be Light

Today's society is inundated with options to experience life quick, fast, and in a hurry. Microwaves, fast food, smart phones, and the Internet all provide opportunities to get something right away. The last thing you want to do is wait. Society teaches you don't have to.

Therefore, it is important to be Kingdom minded. In other words, do not be governed by the dictates of this world. Regardless of what the world says. What does God say? You must wait on the Lord.

Waiting affords many benefits. It enables you to thoroughly examine something before moving forward. You can pray extensively concerning a matter before making a decision. It also helps to determine if what you are seeking is really yours; and allows you to operate with a sound mind, not under pressure.

Patience is a gift from God, not a curse. It is God's way of making sure we receive the best He has to offer. One act of patience may mean a lifetime of peace. That alone, is worth the wait.

Before moving hurriedly, seek God. Is what you desire the will of God? How do you know? Did you receive an answer? Did God confirm His Word? Do you have peace?

If you answered these questions without doubt, all is well. You're on the way to receiving the rewards of patience. You're on the way to receiving God's best. Remember, it's not the end of the world because you didn't receive something right away. Waiting is God's way of giving you something better.

Let's Pray!

Dear Lord. Teach me to be patient. Help me to understand Your ways. Give me the strength to wait on You. Grant me the peace to trust Your perfect will.

In Jesus' name,
Amen

A New Dawn

<u>PEACE</u>

Peace – freedom from or stopping of war; freedom from public disturbance; harmony; absence of mental conflict; calm; quiet; tranquility.

The bible teaches us to live peaceably with everyone, even challenging people. There are times we must take the high road to keep the peace. What does this mean? It means keeping silent even if you're right. It means sacrificing your feelings to save someone else's. It won't always be easy, but you can do it.

The Power of Change

Do you genuinely have peace? If yes, how do you maintain it? If no, when did you lose it?

_____

_____

_____

Where is/will be your environment of peace?

_____

_____

_____

PEACE

Peace I leave with you, my peace I give unto you: not as the world giveth, give I unto you. Let not your heart be troubled, neither let it be afraid.

John 14:27 (KJV)

Thou wilt keep him in perfect peace whose mind is stayed on thee: because he trusteth in thee.

Isaiah 26:3 (KJV)

Let There Be Light

Peace is priceless. It is the most precious commodity one could ever have. There is nothing like it. Everyone wants peace. Unfortunately, not everyone knows how to attain it.

The problem is most don't know what it means to have real peace. Many think it is silence, or the absence of external conflict. Real peace is not merely silence, or the absence of external conflict; it is the absence of internal conflict, as well.

It is possible to achieve peace in the midst of chaotic circumstances. This gives revelation to what Jesus meant in the scriptures. Jesus promised peace to those whose mind is stayed on Him. In other words, keep your mind on Jesus, not on your problems. God wants you to live in peace. Therefore, know it is possible in the midst of difficult circumstances to do so. Some won't understand it. But, the Bible says God's peace surpasses all understanding. It goes beyond what is natural.

With that being said, to be at peace is a choice. There are three ways to accomplish it. First, choose to be at peace with God. It is His promise, if your mind is focused on Him. Second, having peace with God enables you to be at peace, one with another. The Bible says in Hebrews 12:14 to strive for it. When we love God with all of our heart, soul, and mind, we can love one another. God's spirit gives us the grace to do this. Third and finally, peace with God, and peace with one another, fosters internal peace. It is a gift from God. You must guard it with all your heart. When the enemy comes to steal your peace (and he will), *TAKE IT BACK!* As a child of God, peace is rightfully yours. Satan has no dominion over it.

Listen, you can choose to allow circumstances to bother you, or you can decide to rest in God. Choose today to walk in peace. That means not only choosing peace, but deciding to work at it as well. It may not happen right away, but it is possible. It's going to take time. Peace is your promise from God. He made it available to you.

Let's Pray!

Jehovah Shalom, The Lord our Peace. You have given the gift of peace. Help me to receive it. Help me to walk in it. Help me to rest in You. Above all, thank you for being *my* peace.

In Jesus' name,
Amen

PERSEVERANCE

Perseverance – continue in some effort, course, or action despite difficulty and opposition; steadfast in purpose.

Perseverance is paramount to being strong in the Lord. It is the ability to face danger and conquer insurmountable odds. Not everyone has the strength to persevere. Those gifted to do so are tested beyond measure. They have been tried in the fire. They are born to overcome.

The Power of Change

Does perseverance come easy to you?

_____

_____

_____

_____

How do you persevere?

_____

_____

_____

_____

PERSEVERENCE

Therefore put on God's complete armor, that you may be able to resist and stand your ground on the evil day [of danger], and, having done all [the crisis demands], to stand [firmly in your place].

Ephesians 6:13 (AMP)

Let There Be Light

Has God ever given you an assignment that seemed impossible? Did you set out to accomplish the task and somehow you found yourself distracted? Were your goals unreasonable, particularly after you encountered so much difficulty? If your answer is yes, welcome to the world of perseverance.

The ability to persevere is not common to everyone. Only a select few seem to master it. Those able to persevere come from all walks of life. There is no regard to race, culture, or gender. Perseverance is for the one willing to receive, and stand strong, regardless of popularity, acceptance, or personal gain.

It's been said, *"only the strong survive"*. So, how is strength measured? Is it one's physical attributes? Absolutely not! It has everything to do with a determination to complete an assignment. The importance lies in finishing the task, rather than in the obstacles along the way. Yes, there will be obstacles. These obstacles may be subtle or overt. There is no way around them. Confront and learn to handle them. Do not worry. You will make it. Keep your eyes on God. Remain steadfast. Press forward. As you press, victory will come!

Let's Pray!

Dear God. Without You I am nothing. I need You. I need Your strength. Help me to persevere through life's difficulties. Enable me to be a living example to others.

In Jesus' name,
Amen

A New Dawn

PRESSURE

Pressure – harassment; oppression; the constraining or compelling force or influence.

Life can be so unfair. Trials don't have an expected time of arrival. They can happen at any moment. Pray the wisdom of God's "Word" against your burdens. As He delivers you, take that experience and help someone else.

The Power of Change

Where do you feel the most pressure?

_____

_____

_____

_____

With whom have you shared your burdens/pressures?

_____

_____

_____

_____

PRESSURE

No test or temptation that comes your way is beyond the course of what others have had to face. All you need to remember is that God will never let you down; he'll never let you be pushed past your limit; he'll always be there to help you come through it.

1 Corinthians 10:13 (MSG)

Let There Be Light

Life can be unfair. On a daily basis, there's one problem after the next. Stress levels rise as you try to determine best solutions. Interestingly enough, many of the problems encountered aren't yours. Guess what? You're not alone. The pressures of life challenge many. They can be so great; there's room for little else, including your sanity.

Speaking of sanity, have you heard about *"The Club"*? *The Club* is the place where real life happens. It is a place of testing during times of adversity, and crazy things occur at any given moment.

The Club is not for everyone. It has exclusive membership. The cost of inclusion is very high. This cost covers sacrifices, obligations, commitments, and responsibilities. It's enough to make you change your mind. As a very popular commercial states, **"Membership has its privileges!"**

Today's scripture speaks about the tests and temptations anyone can face. It's personal. But God reassures He won't let you down. He works diligently to carry you through every problem, situation, circumstance, and trial. He *will* see you through.

With this in mind, do not fret. You are in the best hands possible. Now, take a deep breath. What trials are you facing? Assess your situation. This will help you to effectively overcome them. Trust God to develop in you a strong, firm, and steadfast spirit. Don't allow pressure to be a threat. Make pressure an opportunity to ...**be strong in the Lord and in the power of His might.** (Ephesian 6:10, KJV) This will help you bring glory and honor to God. As a result, He will show others through you; ...**with God, all things are possible.** (Matthew 19:26, KJV)

Let's Pray!

Almighty God. I bow before Your presence. Send help when life becomes overwhelming. Enable me to stand under pressure. Let the glory of Your presence reign, and grant peace in the time of need.

In Jesus' name,
Amen

A New Dawn

<u>PRIDE</u>

Pride - a high or inordinate opinion of one's own dignity, importance, merit, or superiority, whether as cherished in the mind or as displayed in bearing, conduct, etc.

Never be too proud to admit you need help. People should not be expected to read your mind. Admitting you need help is not a sign of weakness. It is a sign of strength. It means you have courage. Saying you're ok when you're not makes life difficult for you, not others.

The Power of Change

Where do you need the most help in your life?

_____

_____

_____

_____

With whom, can you confide in?

_____

_____

_____

_____

PRIDE

Pride lands you flat on your face; humility prepares you for honors.

Proverbs 29:23 (MSG)

Let There Be Light

I had the pleasure of talking to an awesome woman a few years ago. She has worked in Corporate America, is on the Board of a number of organizations, has strong business savvy, and is very knowledgeable about the health care industry.

Our time together was quite enjoyable as I learned much about her. However, despite all I learned, the one thing that captured my attention was her humility. During our conversation, she was not boastful. Her demeanor was never arrogant or egotistical. Her respect and love for God was paramount, and she had a humble spirit. Having been in the presence of so many people, this was very refreshing.

Some people have an over exaggerated opinion of themselves. They think the world revolves around them. Such an opinion leaves no room for anyone else. There are three reasons why. One, they are self-absorbed. Two, they can't see greatness in others. And three, they're spiritually blind to God's activity in their lives. As a result, He is not glorified.

God must come before everyone and everything else. The Bible says, "***For in him we live and move and have our being.***" (Acts 17:28, NIV) We are sustained by His mercy and grace alone. Only a fool would fail to recognize the goodness of the Lord as each day unfolds.

It's time to honor God in all things. Humility is the key. Do not let pride sabotage your blessings. The repercussions of pride are very painful. They are destructive and cause many to fall from grace. Be an example. Show others God's presence and His delight in your well-being.

Let's Pray!

Eternal God, All power and authority is in Your hands. Help me to remember I'm Your vessel. I am because of You. Keep me ever so humble. You are to be exalted above all.

In Jesus' name,
Amen

PURPOSE

Purpose – the object for which something exists or is done.

As long as you're alive, you can discover your purpose. Now's the time to find it. It's never too late. Never. Who knows? What you have to offer may be perfect for such a time as this.

The Power of Change

Do you know who you are?

_____

_____

_____

_____

Do you know why you're here?

_____

_____

_____

_____

PURPOSE

To everything there is a season, and a time to every purpose under the heaven:

Ecclesiastes 3:1 (KJV)

Let There Be Light

If we understand the meaning of purpose, we know there's a reason why everything exists. Absolutely nothing exists for which there is no purpose. If it's been created, there's a reason for it.

As recorded in the book of Genesis, God spoke heaven and earth into existence. This was not a random act. He knew exactly what He was doing and why. The sun was created to provide daylight; the moon and stars to illuminate the night; herb-bearing seed for food; and oceans, rivers, lakes and streams to provide water. Everything was created for a purpose, even people. Psalm 139 speaks of God's knowledge of us. He knows everything. He especially knows why we exist.

People that don't know their purpose are miserable. Their lives are mediocre and meaningless. When others fulfill their purpose, they are resentful, jealous and irritable. **THIS IS NOT THE WILL OF GOD!** It is your responsibility to seek God concerning your purpose. You must have wise counsel to provide direction, but the ultimate discovery must be yours.

Once you discover your purpose, determine to proceed forward. Pray as never before for revelation. Know you were created for greatness. This greatness goes far beyond your imagination. It is so awesome you'll need God's power to carry it out.

Now live life to the glory of God. As you work to fulfill your purpose, God will give you understanding. It will unfold like a beautiful flower, blooming in the right season. Doors of opportunity will open and you will move in the perfect will of God. Do not put it off another moment. Do not live another day of mere existence. Live life to the fullest. Live life on purpose!

Let's Pray!

God of grace and glory, in humble submission I come. You have created me for a specific purpose. Help me to fulfill it. Connect me to the right people, places, and things. May all line up with Your perfect will. Send help when I veer off course. Help me to always look to You.

In Jesus' name,
Amen

A New Dawn

<u>REDEMPTION</u>

Redemption – deliverance; rescue; repurchase as of something sold.

Redemption is not just a process between God and man. Sometimes there are human relationships that must be redeemed. Get right with your brother or sister. We are better together than apart.

The Power of Change

Recall the last time God redeemed you from something.

_____

_____

_____

_____

Is there one person that you can redeem?

_____

_____

_____

_____

REDEMPTION

For God made Christ, who never sinned, to be the offering for our sin, so that we could be made right with God through Christ.

2 Corinthians 5:21 (NLT)

Let There Be Light

Sometimes there are things we cannot fix. Falling out with someone and trying to make it right, doesn't always work. No matter what you say, the situation can get worse. It makes no difference who's right or wrong. Relationships can be very challenging to repair, even if you say or do all the right things.

Jesus was excellent at fixing things. One word spoken changed many lives. He healed the sick, raised the dead, and freed the bound. It was the nature of His calling. Jesus was sent to earth to bring a dying, rebellious, apostate world back to God. He was the only willing, and able, vessel to bring redemption to humankind.

Due to Adam and Eve's disobedience, humankind suffered a broken relationship with God. The only way to repair it was through the death and suffering of Jesus Christ. Jesus' willingness to bring redemption to humankind was unprecedented. His submission to God gave all an opportunity to receive everlasting life. It could only come through Him.

Redemption is a **free** gift from God. It is not earned. It is given on the premise it would be accepted. All who receive the gift of redemption gain the liberty to walk in the blessings of God.

86

As children of God, we must take what Christ has done seriously. We must appreciate His unwillingness for any to perish and get to know the love of God for all.

God's love is one of unfailing commitment. It aids, sustains, intercedes, supports, and comforts during the most difficult times. It sticks with you to the bitter end. It is a love of mercy and grace, a love like no other. It is the love of **redemption**.

Let's Pray!

God of this Universe, I give you glory. None can compare to You. Thank you for the gift of Jesus Christ. Thank you for uncompromising love. Thank you for the love of redemption that brought me to Your grace and everlasting life.

In Jesus' name,
Amen

A New Dawn

REJECTION

Rejection - to refuse to accept someone or something; rebuff.

Being rejected does not feel good. It affects your sense of self-worth. Feelings of inadequacy begin to invade your thought process. Before sinking into a state of depression, analyze the rejection. Don't be so quick to think it has something to do with you.

The Power of Change

Recall the last time that you felt rejected.

_____

_____

_____

_____

Could this be an opportunity for you to forgive the person who made you feel rejected?

_____

_____

_____

_____

> ## REJECTION
>
> However, those the Father has given me will come to me, and I will never reject them.
> ### John 6:37 (NLT)

Let There Be Light

No one likes to be rejected. To be rejected means to be shut out, cut off, and turned away. It is one of the most difficult experiences a person can have. When someone is rejected, a multitude of emotions come forth. Feelings of abandonment, self-pity, and isolation begin to take over. At any given moment you may face rejection. However, it's important to realize being rejected is not what counts. How you handle the rejection is what matters.

Most people receive rejection as something negative. We are embarrassed and find it difficult to discuss. Rejection is not necessarily bad. Sometimes, rejection is the best thing that can happen. Sure you had your heart set on something that didn't materialize; and being rejected didn't fit into your five-year plan. But, trust me, it's not the end of the world.

Some years ago I sat in the presence of a very powerful preacher. I heard him say something that changed my life. I often think of it when challenged with rejection. He spoke these simple words. *"Rejection leads to direction."* Yes, that's right. Rejection leads to direction. These words began to liberate me. I never looked at rejection the same way. I learned rejection could

90

work for your good. It doesn't always have to mean being shut out. Rejection can also mean protection. It is sometimes God's way of shielding you from going into the wrong direction. Rejection is God's "GPS" (God's Protective System) that navigates you towards purpose.

There are times we think we have it all under control. We believe we know more than God. We are excited about potential opportunities. However, some opportunities may appear fantastic, but they may not be fantastic for you. Stop looking at everyone else. Things aren't always as they seem. Everyone's journey is not the same. Fix your eyes on God.

As you pray for God to govern your life, expect Him to answer at unexpected or inopportune moments. Learn to go with the flow. Remember this. Rejection will come from many directions, but God will **never** reject you. He is faithful to His Word and promises. Be encouraged today and allow God to heal you from rejection. Although painful, it may be necessary. Learn to take the bitter with the sweet. By doing so, you will find that sometimes what's bitter is not so bad after all.

Let's Pray!

Lord God. I confess my pain from rejection. I have become bitter, and I have hurt others. Help me to understand You know what's best for me. Thank you for intercepting the wiles of the enemy. I am grateful Your plan for my life has not been stopped. I yield to Your will.

In Jesus' name,
Amen

RELATIONSHIP

Relationship – a connection, association, or involvement.

Relationship is everything. It is the core of all we say and do. Protect your relationships. What you do now may speak later.

The Power of Change

What positive relationships do you currently have?
[List the person(s)].

_____

_____

How do these relationships benefit you?

_____

_____

What toxic relationships do you currently have?

_____

_____

How do these relationships harm you?

_____

_____

> ## RELATIONSHIP
>
> How good and pleasant it is when God's people live together in unity!
>
> ### Psalm 133:1 (NIV)

Let There Be Light

Relationships can be simple or complex. We experience them on every level. There are family, working, community, professional, emotional, physical, and spiritual relationships, just to name a few. Life does not exist without relationships. It is impossible. At some point, you will have a relationship; whether desired or not.

God is the Author of relationships. From the very beginning, He recognized the need for human connections. The first relationship was established with Adam. The second relationship was between Adam and Eve. These relationships were not created haphazardly. God had reasons for them both.

When God created Adam, He wanted someone in His image and likeness to worship and obey Him, and care for the earth. The relationship was to be harmonious with God, as the Sovereign One, providing for all of Adam's needs.

The relationship between Adam and Eve was different. Although they were both created in the image and likeness of God, there were other reasons for their relationship. God gave specific instructions to be fruitful and multiply. In order to do this, they had to walk in unity, while caring for all that God had given them. Just as God put Adam and Eve together, He wants to do the same for us. Look at the following, concerning the relationship between Adam and Eve:

First, God created Adam and Eve with a **purpose**. It is the reason for existence. Everything and everyone has a purpose. It is your responsibility to discover your purpose. In other words, why are you here?

Second, each relationship must have **unity**. The power of agreement brings forth great things. When we are in agreement, God can accomplish much. There are no limits to what can be done. However, this is not so where there is division. Division brings chaos and sets a continual cycle of disorder.

Third, each relationship must have **direction**. Where are you going? Is the person you are connected to helping you get there, and vice versa? Many are tied to relationships going nowhere. They are miserable yet find it difficult to terminate them. They are controlled by habit. Right or wrong, habit causes you to attach to something that may not be good for you.

These three elements (purpose, unity and direction) are components of a God ordained relationship. They are necessary for healthy cohabitation; and especially important for, although not limited to, male/female relationships. Maintaining a relationship with God helps you in your relationships with others. Your relationships with others won't always be perfect. But, if God is the Author; they will work, and the purpose will be served.

Take the time to examine your relationships. Make sure they meet the requirements mentioned above. See where they fall short. Consult God. Determine the remedy. Review the above-mentioned scripture reference again. *"**How good and pleasant it is when God's people live together in unity.**"* For this to happen, the right people, places, and things must be present and aligned.

Let's Pray!

Father, You know all things. I desire to walk in the relationships You've prepared for me. Help me to discern my connections. Help me to trust Your alliances. Let my relationships be a reflection of Your glory as we accomplish the work of the Kingdom together.

In Jesus' name,
Amen

<u>RESTORATION</u>

Restoration – reinstatement in a former position, rank; restitution for loss, damage; a putting or bringing back into a former, normal, or unimpaired state or condition; reestablish.

God has a plan for your life. He wants you to fulfill it. Sometimes life gets in the way and we miss the plan of God. As a result, we end up making choices that don't fit with His plan. One moment in time can change everything. There is a blessing. The God of grace and glory can fix it. He can make everything wrong, right.

The Power of Change

Was there ever a time when you felt like you were off track (outside of God's plan for your life)?

If so, how did you know? What did you feel?

_____

_____

_____

How did God keep you and get you back on track?

_____

_____

_____

RESTORATION

And I will give you back the crops the locusts ate, my great destroying army that I sent against you. Once again you will have all the food you want. Praise the Lord who does these miracles for you. Never again will my people experience disaster such as this. And you will know that I am here among my people Israel, and that I alone am the Lord, your God. And my people shall never again be dealt a blow like this.

Joel 2:25-27 (LB)

Let There Be Light

I have some friends who are very creative. They have an eye for bringing the best out of the plainest things. They see what average people don't. Colors, patterns, and accents are their specialty; and creating something different is a common desire they all share.

One of the things my friends enjoy doing is home décor. Their ability to put things together well is an understatement. Sometimes it calls for making something new, out of something old. In other words, the old furniture must be restored. Restoration brings to surface hidden beauty not previously realized.

Oftentimes, restoration is necessary for God's people. When we move outside His perfect will, it is important to get back on course. Just like old furniture, God wants to restore His people. He knows better than anyone, what lies beneath the surface. He also knows better than anyone, what it takes to bring it out.

Biblical history consistently reveals Israel's disobedience, and the need for constant intervention. Time and time again, Israel made promises to God that were not kept. Time and time again, God's grace, mercy, and forgiveness prevailed on their behalf.

In today's scripture, God speaks to Israel. He informs them that change is coming. A change is coming so great; it will overturn the decision brought against them concerning their demise. There will be a restoration of all things; and they will never experience loss of this magnitude again.

Perhaps you suffered losses and felt like it was all over. Years of frustration have caused you to believe there is no way out. Just like Israel, your situation doesn't have to be permanent. The same God Who promised restoration to Israel, is the same God Who will bring restoration to you. Allow this same God, Who delivered Israel, to deliver you. He wants you in your rightful place. Your set time is only a prayer away. Trust Him with all your heart; and receive the blessing of restoration. He wants to give you the desires of your heart.

Let's Pray!

Faithful God. I have fallen out of Your will. Restore me to my rightful place. I want to follow Your plan. Let me be a living testimony of Your goodness.

In Jesus' name,
Amen

<u>STEADFAST</u>

Steadfast – firmly fixed in place or position.

In order to be steadfast, one must have great discipline. You must have the ability to stay the course, no matter what. Put your hand to the plow. Proceed full speed ahead.

The Power of Change

What do you believe God for right now?

_____

_____

_____

_____

Are you committed to the journey?

_____

_____

_____

_____

STEADFAST

Therefore, my beloved brethren, be ye steadfast, unmovable, always abounding in the work of the Lord, for ye know that your labor is not in vain in the Lord.

1 Corinthians 15:58 (KJV)

Let There Be Light

Standing firm in your faith is a desirable character trait. The ability to stand in the midst of opposition, isolation, and despair calls for great strength. It has nothing to do with physical prowess, but has everything to do with being rooted and grounded in what you believe. It's knowing what you believe will happen. You may not know how; you may not know when; but you know *it will* happen.

Having the fortitude and strength to believe, only comes from situations where faith is tested; perhaps, even tried in the fire of life. You may be faced with insurmountable obstacles; however, the capacity to stay the course is paramount.

In order to stay the course, it's necessary to wear blinders to stay focused. Once you make a decision to do this, expect distractions from everywhere. Distractions will come as false emergencies, well-meaning requests, and unwritten obligations. They will foster guilt and obligation, to something, or someone, under the wrong pretense. You must be on guard.

The above scripture brings to light the importance of being steadfast. The storms of life will come. They may hit hard;

yet, because you are "...**strong in the Lord and the power of His might**," (Ephesians 6:10, KJV) you will not be moved. Life will make you think your efforts to succeed will result to no avail. Not so. Opposition only comes when something is worth the fight.

Staying the course is hard work, but don't give up. Your labor is not in vain. There is value in hard work. Hard work means great rewards. No, I am not talking about Heaven. There are rewards before you get to Heaven. As you "...**live and move and have our being...**" (Acts 17:28, KJV) in God, He will direct your paths. True obedience will position you for blessings. Stay focused. Determine not to allow the issues of life to throw you off course. Use these issues to strengthen your resolve, and empower you. Yes, be **steadfast**! It will pay off in the end.

Let's Pray!

Lord. All praise to Your name. Give me the strength to remain steadfast to carry out Your will. Let my life of grace be a witness to others.

In Jesus' name,
Amen

TRANSITION

Transition – passing from one condition, stage, activity, place to another.

Transition is a major part of life. It calls for movement. Education, a new home, job, and family all play a part of transition. Know that transition is necessary. It is the result of change.

The Power of Change

Are you currently going through a transition?

_____

_____

Do you have the faith required to get you to the other side?

_____

_____

Why is this transition necessary?

_____

_____

_____

TRANSITION

God told Abram: Leave your country, your family, and your father's home for a land that I will show you. I'll make you a great nation and bless you. I'll make you famous; you'll be a blessing. I'll bless those who bless you; those who curse you I'll curse. All the families of the Earth will be blessed through you.

Genesis 12:1-3 (MSG)

Let There Be Light

God introduces us to Abram, the son of Terah, in the Book of Genesis at the end of chapter eleven. He becomes a man, marries Sarai, and his family settles in a place called Haran. Later, his father Terah dies, and God tells Abram to follow His command and move.

Seasons of life dictate change. God is a master of orchestrating change, particularly when it connects to His divine plan. In the twelfth chapter of Genesis, God tells Abram to leave his country and people, and go to a land He will show him. This could not have been easy. God was telling Abram to leave familiar surroundings and go to a place of which he was not familiar.

Can you imagine? You are settled in a nice place. Everything seems to be going just fine, and then you must leave. You are told *you will be the father of a great nation; you will be blessed, and you will be a blessing. Those that bless you will be blessed; and those that curse you will be cursed. The entire world will be blessed because of you.* That's a lot to handle. That's a lot to swallow.

Not many people are like Abram. There would be a barrage of questions fired at God. After that, another round would be released. Would you be willing to listen to God and obey? Would you be willing to step out on faith, no questions asked… just go? Would you trust God's leading to a place you know nothing about? Let's face it. It takes great faith to do so.

Just as God spoke to Abram, He speaks through situations, circumstances, people, and events. He is not limited to one way of doing things. As your relationship with Him grows, there will be times your faith is tested. Sometimes it will be easy. Other times it will not.

We are living during a time of great spiritual transition. Major shifts are taking place in the Body of Christ. God is uprooting, repositioning, and making changes that impact our daily living. These changes are affecting ministries, employment, communities, families, etc. Change is everywhere. The beauty of it all is some will experience major change, after years and years of sowing seed through much prayer, trial, and tribulation. The promises of restoration are now breaking forth. It is a time of restitution for the faithful few. The arrival of our transition is the fruit of hard labor, ushering in a great harvest. God is faithful! It doesn't matter how long something takes. God will come through.

As you experience the outpouring of God's Spirit during this time, remember transition is imminent. It is what's called for in this hour. It is your just reward. Look for the beauty of God's glory. He is faithful. You will see Him in an awesome way. Give God praise! The set time to favor you has come.

Let's Pray!

Dear Lord, thank You for a new day with new opportunities. Help me to understand these opportunities as transition. Open my eyes to see this as growth and show me Your perfect will.

In Jesus' name,
Amen

TRUST

Trust – firm belief or confidence; anticipation; hope; rely or depend on.

Real trust must be unconditional. Oftentimes, it's not easy; but it's necessary. Trust for one another is paramount to Kingdom work. We can't work together unless there is trust. But, it won't happen unless you learn to trust God. Trusting Him makes the difference. Trusting Him helps in our relationships with one another. Trusting Him will cause everything to fall into place.

The Power of Change

On scale of 1 to 10 (be honest), what is your trust level with God?

_____

_____

Based on your answer, why do you think it is so hard *or* easy to trust God?

_____

_____

Write out a list of 3 things that he did for you in the last month.

_____

_____

TRUST

God's way is perfect. All the Lord's promises prove true. He is a shield for all who look to him for protection.

2 Samuel 22:31 (NLT)

Let There Be Light

The most valuable thing in any relationship is trust. It is the glue that holds everything together. Trust ensures cohesiveness when nothing else is left. Without trust, relationships falter under the challenges of fidelity, dependability, and hope. Trust provides the stability necessary to weather any storm, and ride the waves of adversity designed to destroy them.

Many don't appreciate the value of trust. They don't regard the importance of being loyal. As a result, they miss the benefits of a good solid relationship where love is pure, and the connection is real.

God wants a real relationship of trust with His children. He wants to manifest the impossible; demonstrating His power in such a way, it will leave others speechless. In order to accomplish this, we must believe God's Word. His Word must be the life force that motivates every decision we make. It must govern the course we take and instill the strength necessary to pursue the impossible. We must step out in faith, believing God will make good on His promises. Above all else, we must understand, with God, there are no gray areas. It is either black or white. He does not waiver in between.

Make a decision to trust God. Pray for Him to strengthen, guide, and keep you. Ask for His help when faced with difficult situations. It will be the best decision you've ever made.

Let's Pray!

All wise God, thank you for Your Spirit. You are faithful to Your Word. Help me to remember Your promises. Teach me to trust You through difficult times.

In Jesus' name,
Amen

UNITY

Unity – state of being one; oneness of mind, feeling, etc., as among a number of persons; concord; harmony; agreement.

Being one, puts us on the same playing field. As a result, we're able to accomplish more by working together. That's what good healthy relationships are all about. Let's purpose to work in unity. By doing so, the rewards will be great, and our relationships will be even greater.

The Power of Change

In general, do you have harmonious relationships?

_____

_____

_____

_____

What is one relationship that you would like to see unified? What can you do to ensure that it is?

_____

_____

_____

_____

> **UNITY**
>
> How wonderful, how beautiful, when brothers and sisters get along! It's like costly anointing oil flowing down head and beard, flowing down Aaron's beard, flowing down the collar of his priestly robes. It's like the dew on Mount Hermon flowing down the slopes of Zion. Yes, that's where God commands the blessing, ordains eternal life.
>
> **Psalm 133:1-3 (MSG)**

Let There Be Light

Have you ever attended a band rehearsal? Great care goes into practice. But before practice, the band warms up. Each instrument sounds off independently. Emphasis is placed on making sure the instruments are ready for performance; not how they sound together. As a result, you don't hear beautiful music. You hear noise. The sound is distorted.

Distortion is not soothing to the ear. It is irritating, and harmful to hearing. Unlike harmony, which brings a sense of calm; distortion creates discord. There is no unity. Unity is important if the instruments are going to work together.

Unity is also critical to the Body of Christ. Without it, there's a breakdown. Things are subject to fall apart. It's been said, *"There's strength in numbers"*. Strength comes when we stand collectively; to pursue and achieve the same result.

When God's people are not in unity, we produce noise; just like the instruments in the band, during warm ups. Each

114

person is solely concerned with doing his/her own thing; not taking into consideration what it means to the whole.

We are called to work together. We won't always agree, but we should put differences aside for the common good. Some would say for the sake of the gospel.

We have been created to make beautiful music together. We are only as great as our brothers and sisters. Our focus should be on celebrating and appreciating one another; knowing we are better together than apart. With that, we can do great things. The scripture says unity, *"is like costly anointing oil"* where its value is not measured in dollars and cents. We must work together. By doing so, we will be blessed, and God will be glorified!

Let's Pray!

God of grace and glory, help me to walk in agreement with my brothers and sisters in Christ. Let peace reign as we pursue Kingdom work. Let the spirit of harmony guide our efforts.

In Jesus' name,
Amen

A New Dawn

VISION

Vision – seen by other than normal sight; mental image; ability to perceive something not actually visible.

Vision is the ability to see beyond the scope of what's physically apparent. It is an opportunity to glimpse into your future, real, or perceived. What do you see? What do you want to see?

The Power of Change

What is your vision for the next 3 years?

_____

_____

_____

_____

What do you need for this vision to come to past? Who do you need for it to come to past?

_____

_____

_____

_____

_____

_____

```
┌─────────────────────────────────────────────────────┐
│                      VISION                           │
│                                                       │
│  If people can't see what God is doing, they          │
│  stumble all over themselves; but when they attend    │
│  to what he reveals, they are most blessed.           │
│              Proverbs 29:18 (MSG)                     │
└─────────────────────────────────────────────────────┘
```

Let There Be Light

It's difficult to find your way in the dark. Ask anyone looking for the bathroom in the middle of the night. Stumbling can happen. Even a night light is not always helpful.

Sometimes God's people stumble. This often happens when they are unaware of His activity in their lives. Many could avoid troubling pain; if they sought, trusted, believed, and followed God. But, unfortunately, they're stuck in their own way. They go about here and there; not realizing there's something better.

Being stuck in your own way doesn't leave room for God. When there's no room for God, you miss His vision. When you miss His vision, you're stumbling trying to find your way in the dark. Being in the dark causes you to miss the plan of God. The King James Version of the Bible informs us "*where there is no vision, the people perish*" (Proverbs 29:18). How do you get God's vision? You must go to Him. It takes time. Do not allow impatience to harass you. God knows His timing for everything. I've heard it said, learning to wait is the PHD of maturity in spirit.

If that's the case, many have not received a high school diploma, let alone a PHD!

Know this, anything worth waiting for is worth receiving. God has much in store for you. Your opportunity to receive from Him is based on your ability to see the vision, hear His voice, and respond to His instructions. There is a Divine appointment headed your way. Do not let the lack of vision cause you to miss your moment. You have waited long enough. Open your spiritual eyes and receive your blessing!

Let's Pray!

Almighty God, You see and know all things. There is nothing hidden from You. Manifest Your vision for my life. Grant me clarity to see as You see. Help me not to fear what I don't understand.

In Jesus' name,
Amen

<u>WORRY</u>

Worry – to torment oneself with or suffer from disturbing thoughts; fret.

Did you know that worry is a thief? It robs you of present peace. Why worry about something that might happen? Plans, projects, proposals, and strategies will all come to an end. Just put the work in. Pray and trust God. By faith, he'll work it out. You've got better things to do with your time. So go do them!

The Power of Change

What is the last thing you worried about? How did worrying help the situation?

_____

_____

_____

_____

What can you do differently next time?

_____

_____

_____

_____

_____

WORRY

Therefore I say unto you, take no thought for your life, what ye shall eat, or what ye shall drink; nor yet for your body, what ye shall put on. Is not the life more than meat, and the body than raiment?

Behold the fowls of the air: for they sow not, neither do they reap, nor gather into barns; yet your heavenly Father feedeth them. Are ye not much better than they?

Which of you by taking thought can add one cubit unto his stature?

Wherefore, if God so clothe the grass of the field, which today is, and tomorrow is cast into the oven, shall he not much more clothe you, O ye of little faith?

But seek ye first the kingdom of God and his righteousness; and all these things shall be added unto you.

Matthew 6:25-27, 30-33 (KJV)

Let There Be Light

Worry is the unpleasant monster that comes upon you unawares. It is never alone. Fear and doubt are its traveling companions. The three of them will take you for the ride of your life. Worry is a constant aggravation. It nags and gnaws at you to focus on things out of your control. Constant taunting images replayed in the mind; that present a no-win situation. If that's not enough, the spirit of fear intimidates you into feeling you're suffering from a lost cause. After that, doubt comes to bombard you with question after question, as you waver from one thing to the next. It's an endless cycle.

It is not the intent of God for His children to worry. From the days of Adam and Eve, God has shown Himself to be a provider and sustainer of life. When we surrender to His authority, we will experience His unlimited provision. God will demonstrate His ability to keep what belongs to Him.

Think about what you've seen God do before. Recall to mind experiences of the past that challenged your faith. Remember when you thought it was over? Remember when you thought you couldn't take any more? What did God do? How did He demonstrate His power? You must be strong in the Lord. Remember the words of Caleb when it was time for the children of Israel to take the Promise Land. *"Let us go up at once, and possess it; for we are well able to overcome it."* (Numbers 13:30, KJV)

Caleb and Joshua stood strong in a situation intended to cause fear, worry, and doubt. However, despite all, they believed God. People did not move them. God moved them. What about you? What are you worried about? Why do you worry about something that might happen? Worry does not come from God. We are to be people of faith, trusting and believing in His word.

Let's Pray!

Thank you Lord for grace and mercy. There is no one greater than You. Help me remember the earth is Yours, and its fullness. Today I cast my cares upon You. I choose not to worry. There is no situation You can't handle.

In Jesus' name,
Amen

INVITATION

My sincere hope is that this devotional inspired you, reminded you how much God loves you, and challenged you not to lose hope for your future. We have covered a lot over the past 31 days and I believe that you can now be successful in life with what I've provided. However, the truth is if you don't have Jesus as your Lord and Savior you will never be *truly successful.* You will continue to live life on the hamster's wheel.

Life with Him is not promised to be easy and without trials, but it sure can be a lot smoother if you walk hand in hand with His and step in step with the Savior. I would like to invite you to allow Jesus into your heart and into your life.

Romans 10: 9-10, says, *"If you declare with your mouth, "Jesus is Lord, "and believe in your heart that God raised him from the dead, you will be saved. For it is with your heart that you believe and are justified, and it is with your mouth that you profess your faith and are saved."*

If you just accepted him as Lord and Savior, I want to welcome you into the Body of Christ. You now have new family members, me being one of them! Your life is going to be different and I want to tell you that the angels in heaven are rejoicing with you!

Please find a Bible teaching church in your community and stay connected to me and other like-minded believers.

Congratulations on your **NEW** journey!

REFLECTIONS & AHA MOMENTS

Please write down some of your **Aha moments** from this book and share with me at dawnschristopher@gmail.com. I'd love to hear from you!

Thank you for allowing me to encourage you on this journey called life.

_____

_____

_____

_____

_____

_____

_____

_____

_____

_____

_____